CSX TRANSPORTATION

RICHARD BILLINGSLEY

Dedicated to my pal Simon. When I have a camera in my hand, he is the best gopher in the world. And the worst...

First published 2021

Amberley Publishing
The Hill, Stroud
Gloucestershire, GL5 4EP

www.amberley-books.com

ISBN 978 1 4456 9710 9 (print)
ISBN 978 1 4456 9711 6 (ebook)

British Library Cataloguing in Publication Data.
A catalogue record for this book is available from the British Library.

Origination by Amberley Publishing.
Printed in the UK.

Introduction

Headquartered in the northern Florida city of Jacksonville, CSX Transportation is one of the two Class I railroads covering much of the eastern United States, the other being the Norfolk Southern Railroad.

The CSX operational area extends from Quebec and Ontario in Canada, down through the Northeast Corridor of the United States down to Georgia and Florida in the south, and east to Louisiana, Tennessee, Kentucky and Indiana. The company currently owns and operates around 21,000 route miles of railroad.

Although many of the predecessor railroads have a history that will soon be two centuries old, the first constituent of the modern-day company was moving freight in 1827; the CSX Corporation only came into being in late 1980, formed by the technical merger of the Chessie System with the Seaboard Coast Line. Initially there was little change: new equipment was supplied in the colours of the two constituent railroads and the status quo remained until 1986 when the Seaboard lines changed their name to CSX Transportation. A grey livery was initially used, but this was short-lived as in 1987 a new blue and grey scheme was introduced. Yellow was soon added to this, and various subtle changes over the years have led to the present-day blue and yellow colours.

In 1987, the Chessie System companies merged to form a single unit and that, as the Chesapeake and Ohio Railroad, finally merged into CSX Transportation later that year. The federally owned Conrail System was sold in 1997 after a joint bid by CSX and Norfolk Southern was accepted by the Federal Surface Transport Board with CSX taking around 40 per cent of the assets including nearly 4,000 route miles, predominantly in the north-east. CSX operation of these routes began in the summer of 1999.

Despite a hostile merger attempt by the Canadian Pacific in 2014, CSX Transportation has remained an independent operation owned by the CSX Corporation, a NASDAQ listed company. With tracks in twenty-three US states, two Canadian provinces and the District of Columbia, the 25,000-strong workforce operates around 1,300 trains every day and provides trackage for nearly 200 passenger trains, as well as hosting other railroads operations on its tracks.

CSX connects with over 200 regional and short lines and shares trackage rights with many other railroads. The CSX and Norfolk Southern systems are very much intertwined; both companies share trackage rights agreements and make use of each other's assets in many locations. In common with the other Class I railroads, they also host trains from other systems including BNSF-operated coal trains from the Powder River Basin coalfields in Wyoming and Union Pacific fuel trains from Illinois to Florida.These trains are generally crewed by CSX personnel whilst on CSX tracks.

Day-to-day operations on the network are achieved by use of the Precision Scheduled Railroad concept. This method of operation, introduced by CSX in 2017, uses timetabled scheduling of trains rather than operation as and when required. Intermodal traffic is sometimes combined with other types of traffic on some runs according to traffic needs. This method of operation has undoubtedly improved the financial performance of the railroads that use it – less infrastructure, assets and employees are needed to move the same tonnage of goods – but there has been considerable criticism of some aspects of the concept, not least from customers who feel that their service has been adversely affected or even curtailed. The rail workers unions have also been less than happy as thousands of jobs have disappeared as a result of the new way of working. The Precision Scheduled method has been adopted by most of the Class I railroads, the notable exception being the huge BNSF Railway. A considerable reduction in the locomotive fleet has been achieved as a result of Precision Scheduling. In 2019 there were large numbers of redundant units stored out of use in the yards at Waycross GA, Corbin KY and several other occasions. Many of these locomotives remain in good condition and are likely to see reuse with other railroads.

CSX have also sold off some routes in recent years, notably in Florida where the main route across the Panhandle, the 430-mile line from Baldwin to Pensacola, was sold to Rail USA in 2019 after a rationalisation of CSX service in the region. The line is now a Class III railroad and operates as the Florida Gulf and Atlantic Railroad; remnant traffic retained by CSX now operates via a much longer route further north.

Some of the Florida 'A' line, one of three north to south routes through the state, has also changed owners: the Florida Department of Transport now owns the tracks from DeLand, through Orlando south to Poinciana and operates the regular SunRail commuter service along the 60-mile route. Both CSX and Amtrak retain trackage rights along the route, but most CSX traffic not destined for the Orlando area now uses the 'S' line, much closer to the western Florida Gulf coast. Much of the infrastructure of the Orlando route has been renewed with double-track, enhanced signalling and new passenger stations, but CSX use is generally restricted to times where passenger service is less frequent – generally overnight and at weekends.

This book concentrates on the southern end of the company's operations with many of the pictures taken in Florida, Georgia and Alabama, illustrating a wide variety of the traffic on offer, as well as key operational locations. The pictures date from 2010 up to the late autumn of 2019 in an attempt to illustrate the modern CSX railroad, its equipment and traffic, and its interactions with other railroads. Traffic from Amtrak, Norfolk Southern and SunRail is included, as well as CSX

units that have escaped to destinations far from home.
I hope you enjoy this snapshot of 'How Tomorrow Moves'.

CSX Transportation Locomotive Designations

To the casual viewer who has little knowledge of American railroads, the designations used for differing motive power might seem bewildering. The following notes will help the reader to understand the differing types of locomotives.

For much of the past forty years, the market in the US has been dominated by two manufacturers: Electro-Motive Division (EMD), a General Motors subsidiary until 2005 and now owned by Progress Rail; and General Electric (GE).

Unlike some of the Class I railroads, the CSX Transportation high-horsepower fleet is comprised largely of GE units; only penny numbers of EMD SD60 and 70 designs are used. The split between GE and EMD for lower-powered units is roughly half and half.

The larger of the two manufacturers is General Electric; they currently hold a two-thirds market share. The current Evolution series started production in 2003 and over 5,000 units have been built. Some of the varying types are detailed below:

ES44DC Evolution series, 4400hp, DC traction motors
ES44AC Evolution series, 4400hp, AC traction motors
ES44C4 Evolution series, 4400hp, AC traction motors, A-1-A trucks with centre unpowered axle
ET44AC Tier 4 Evolution, 4400hp, AC traction motors
ET44C4 Tier 4 Evolution, 4400hp, AC traction motors

A letter H at the end of a designation indicates that the locomotive is a ballasted, heavier version with increased tractive adhesion, for example, ET44AH instead of ET44AC. A CTE designation denotes use of controlled tractive equipment, similar to the Sepex motors used in the UK, for example, C45ACCTE. The UK Powerhaul Class 70 PH37ACmi is loosely based on the Evolution platform.

Many locomotives built before the Evolution series remain in use. These include the Dash 8 and Dash 9 series locomotives C40-8W (4000hp Dash 8) and C44-9W (4400hp Dash 9). Both designs utilise DC traction equipment; these were superseded by the AC4400CW locomotives built with AC motors.

The second manufacturer is Electro-Motive. The company has produced locomotives since the 1930s and became the market leader, overtaking the American Locomotive Company (ALCO) in the 1960s. That dominance was lost to General Electric in the late 1980s; EMD however still produces considerable quantities for both domestic and international markets.

The GP (General Purpose) locomotives are four-axle units built from 1949 to 1994 utilising EMD 567, 645 or 710 series engines. Many GPs have been rebuilt for extended service and whilst their days of long-distance, high-speed work are long gone, they are still prolific on local trip workings and yard duty.

The SD (Standard Duty) locomotives are the larger six-axle units built from 1952 onwards using the EMD 265, 567, 645, 710 and 1010 series engines. The SD40 is basically a larger variant of the GP locomotive, but the SD series has evolved to produce large, high-powered units such as the SD70ACe, in production since 2003. The Union Pacific is a large EMD customer; over 1,500 of the 4000hp SD70Ms were purchased by the railroad.

The designations on EMD locomotives differ to those on GE locomotives in that the numberings (SD40, SD60, etc.) refer to individual models rather than engine output. SD units up to the SD60M and SD70M used DC motors; the SD60MAC and SD70MAC were the first to offer AC equipment. The SD70MAC was replaced in 2003 by the SD70Ace, which is now the standard EMD heavy-hauler; its latest guise is the SD70ACe-T4, which complies with Tier 4 emissions legislation.

Running alongside Railroad Avenue in Garden City AL, GE ES44AH #3101 leads a pair of GE AC4400CW locomotives still wearing the old 'Bright Future' paint scheme on a southbound coal working. Captured on 4 October 2019, the train recessed overnight in nearby Birmingham before continuing east.

Golden late afternoon sun shines down on Folkston GA on 26 September 2019 as a southbound train of auto-racks passes through the compact downtown area of the city. The train is led by two GE Evolution units, ES44AH #886 and ES40DC #5464. Both locomotives entered service with CSX in 2007.

The modern face of CSX is represented by GE ES44AH #913, leading a coal train through Kissimmee FL on 24 September 2019. Differing from the manufacturer's designation, CSX classifies the entire 300-strong batch of these locomotives, which date from 2007 to 2011, as CW44AHs.

Standing on the St John's River, the Florida city of Jacksonville is home to the headquarters of CSX Transportation. The offices occupy a prime location looking over the river – ironically the drawbridge below the Acosta Freeway Bridge carries the tracks of the Florida East Coast railroad over the water. A Skyway train passes over the median on 24 January 2012.

With the flags of the Union and the State of Georgia flying high, ES40DC #5386 brings another train of auto-racks from the Waycross line through Folkston on 9 October 2019. Only the front two of the four locomotives are under power; the other two units are being moved to Baldwin Yard for duty from there.

Just a few yards from the previous picture, this wonderful Baltimore and Ohio caboose provides trackside-themed holiday accommodation for the railfan visiting Folkston. The Baltimore and Ohio existed for 159 years before its 1987 merge in the Chesapeake and Ohio, the Chessie System, and eventually CSX.

Another railroad that formed part of the modern-day CSX system was the Nashville, Chattanooga and St Louis Railroad. After several mergers and takeovers, the railroad was incorporated into the Seaboard System which eventually formed part of the new CSX company. This caboose is displayed in the middle of the city of Bridgeport AL.

With over 20,000 route miles, the CSX maintenance of way teams are constantly kept busy repairing and renewing track, structures and signalling. Wherever possible, track maintenance is mechanised to improve efficiency. These machines parked at Orlando FL on 2 June 2011 had been utilised in recent work in the downtown area.

Despite rationalisation in the motive power fleet, CSX still retains considerable numbers of smaller locomotives which can still be seen on long-distance work. EMD SD40-3 #4025 and SD40-2 #8368 approach Waycross GA from the south on 27 September 2019, with a manifest train for the classification yard.

High-horsepower locomotives meet CSX hardware at Folkston GA on 26 September 2019. Both the intermodal container and the locomotive, ET44AH #3407, carry the current version of CSX house colours, known as 'Dark Future', with the latest 'boxcar' logo introduced in 2011.

Standing alongside the single track of the route north from Mobile to Montgomery AL, Atmore Amtrak station looks tidy and ready to serve passengers. Sadly, no train has called since the discontinuation of service on the Sunset Limited west of New Orleans in 2005 after damage to the tracks caused by Hurricane Katrina. Photographed on 7 October 2019.

Tracks were quickly restored for freight service to resume after the hurricane. Just a few yards south of the former Amtrak station in the previous picture, a Mobile-bound manifest disturbs the relative quiet of midday in Atmore. Traffic along the route has increased with the diversion of traffic from the now sold Gulf Coast route.

A few moments later, the three-unit train passes under the tracks of the Alabama and Gulf Coast Railway to the south of Atmore. To the right and behind the train, a single-track curve links the two lines. Despite being equipped with modern signalling, the curve is overgrown and sees little, if any, use.

The original version of the 'Dark Future' livery, carried by SD40-3 #4023, featured the then standard CSX corporate lettering. The newer 'boxcar' logo is carried by #4063 behind. UK readers will see similarities here with the much-lamented British Rail blue era.

Locomotive #2774 is an EMD GP38-2 dating from June 1978 and originally Conrail #8195. Seen at Auburndale FL on 24 September 2019, the locomotive was parked on a short spur after engaging in a day's switching to nearby factories.

AC4400CW #413 poses for the camera at Montgomery AL on 5 October 2019. The locomotive has carried the YN2 'Bright Future' livery from new in 1999; the 'flash' below the number indicates the loco has AC traction motors. Note again that CSX have used a differing designation to the manufacturer, this time CW44AC.

More detail, this is the blunt end of EMD GP38-2 #2641, parked at Sanford FL on 29 May 2011. The loco is painted in the YN3 'Dark Future' colours but retains the original CSX logo. #2641 looks tidy – many units of its age carry differing number fonts on the panels and paint that has done many years of service.

ES44AH #3168 looks the part approaching the dockland area of Mobile AL on 7 October 2019, leading a manifest heading north-east. Delivered new to CSX in 2013, the locomotive still carries pristine, albeit dusty, YN3 'Dark Future' livery with the 'boxcar' logo, introduced in 2011.

Back in January 2012 it was still a little too soon to see the 'boxcar' logo in regular use. GE C40-8W #7533 leads an ES44AH and an EMD MP15T switcher south through Folkston GA on the 23rd of that month. #7533, in common with many other C40-8W units, was retired from service in 2018 and sold for further use.

ES40DC #5320 waits at Manchester GA with a southbound maintenance of way train, 30 September 2019. The lack of a 'flash' logo immediately distinguishes the loco as a DC-motored unit. CSXT is the railroad's AAR (American Association of Railroads) reporting mark. These are used to denote ownership of locos and stock.

For many years, the Tropicana Juice train from Florida to New Jersey was renowned for its high-horsepower traction and fast schedule – the fruit carried in its refrigerated cars was obviously a time-sensitive cargo. The unit train no longer runs, and the fruits now travel on other trains such as this northbound manifest.

Crossing the Tennessee River at Decatur AL, this magnificent lift bridge carries CSX trains on the main line from Nashville TN to Birmingham AL. Although most trains over the bridge are CSX operated, the bridge is actually owned by the Norfolk Southern, whose line from Chattanooga TN also crosses here.

The lifting span is crossed by Birmingham-bound CSX coal on 4 October 2019. Most views seen of the bridge are from the east – industrial activity on the riverbank on the west side makes access impossible. The bridge is relatively modern and was constructed in 1978–79 to replace a swing bridge in the same location.

The need for a lifting section becomes obvious; even the pleasure cruiser on the right would not otherwise fit. The tug to the left is one of those used to pull the long sand barges, one of which is moored behind the two craft.

With the lifting section up, one of the frequent sand barges passes under the tracks. The whole process takes less than five minutes; lifting and lowering of the deck is completed after around one minute. Despite this, it is common to see one mode of transport delaying another.

CSX-branded intermodal containers cross one of the fixed girders on the south bank. Unlike the other Class Is, CSX own and operate many of these containers. Most containers are leased to or owned by shipping companies such as Schneider's or JB Hunt.

Undisturbed by the two growling ES44AHs just yards away, a heron wades through the shallower waters of the Tennessee. These pictures were taken on 3 and 4 of October 2019. At the time Alabama was enjoying an exceptionally warm autumn with afternoon temperatures up into the nineties.

The heat is perhaps a little too much for the crew of ex-Baltimore and Ohio GP40-2 #6246 as it reaches dry land – the conductor's cab door is open for a little extra ventilation! This train is near its destination: Decatur Yard lies just a couple of miles south.

A final view of the lifting span shows the structures that enclose the huge counterweights used to move the lifting deck. Access to the maintenance and control building midway across the bridge looks to be a process not intended for the faint-hearted.

The CSX yard at Decatur lies to the south of the city. Although it is located in an industrial area, plenty of greenery surround the tracks. GP40-2 #6987 and Road Slug #2387 switch tanks on 3r October 2019. Road Slugs are former locomotives with the diesel engine removed used to provide adhesion weight. Power to the Slug's traction motors is provided by the GP40-2.

GP locomotives in the sunset at Decatur AL on 3 October 2019. Despite only being a small facility, there was considerable activity here during the long, golden sunset, with two loco sets switching separate tank trains.

Testament to their success, EMD's GP series locomotives have been used for well over half a century. There are many different configurations, and many have been rebuilt, but the basic design remains. All four of the units pictured here have seen at least forty-two years' service and are likely to see a good few more.

A comparison of cabs at Decatur AL, 3 October 2019. Thirty years separate GP40-2 #6142, new to the Baltimore and Ohio in 1975, and ES40DC #5237, new to CSX in 2005, the first design of the now universal Evolution series locomotive.

Seen previously, #6987 and Slug #2387 a little later in the evening. The modifications to the Slug unit are evident, with no diesel engine to cool the fans and radiators now gone. The cab and controls are retained to allow the formation to be driven from either end.

With just a few moments left before the sun sinks beyond the horizon, golden light picks out some of the finer details as #s 6987 and 2387 back down a central yard road with their now assembled train of tanks. The pair disappeared behind the sidings full of cars moments later.

Another 2005 ES40DC, #5246, spent the evening parked adjacent to the yard offices at the north end of Decatur Yard. Perhaps a little too large to be used on local work, the loco and sister #5237 behind would likely be assigned to a main-line job the next day.

Moving south-east into Central Florida, the Orlando-Kissimmee area is known worldwide as a major tourist destination. Using CSX tracks, Amtrak's Silver Service trains from Miami to New York serve both cities, providing twice daily service along the Eastern Seaboard. Scruffy-looking GE Genesis P42DC #164 calls at Kissimmee on its long journey north on 16 January 2012.

ES44AH #3119 brings the rear of a coal train heading for the Curtis H. Stanton power generation plant through Kissimmee on 24 September 2019. The tracks here are now owned by the Florida Department of Transport and daytime CSX movements are unusual.

SunRail is a Florida state initiative, using 60 miles of the former CSX 'A' line between DeBary and Poinciana. The line has been virtually rebuilt since purchase in 2014, with new signalling, tracks and stations. Service is provided by Motive Power Industries MP32PH-Q locomotives. #101 heads north at Kissimmee on 24 September 2019.

The new SunRail station at Kissimmee lies immediately north of the existing Amtrak facility. Stations are unstaffed but have constant CCTV monitoring, information points and ticket machines that accept both cash and card. A southbound calls on 24 September 2019.

Back in the days of CSX ownership of the route, AC4400CW #351 threads an intermodal through downtown Orlando and approaches the Amtrak station in the Medical District. The 20,000-seat Amway Center, home to the Orlando Magic basketball team, looms in the distance. 4 June 2011.

The splendid, if slightly jaded, Atlantic Coast Lines station at Orlando has served the city since 1926. Today, the station hosts Amtrak's Silver Service trains as well as SunRail commuter services. The New York-bound Silver Star calls on 2 June 2011, led by P42DC's #s 5 and 62. The journey to New York Penn from here is around twenty-two hours.

Back at Kissimmee, the southbound Silver Star is still around seven hours away from its Miami destination. Led by P42DC #205 and P40DC #816, the train will next call at Lakeland, nearly an hour's ride. The new tracks as a result of the SunRail project are evident in the foreground on 24 September 2019.

SunRail has a fleet of twenty Bombardier bi-level passenger cars, thirteen of which are cab cars. The cars usually lead northbound with the MP32PH-Q locomotive pushing at the rear. As ridership increases, further trailer cars are available as an add-on option to the original order. Car #2005 approaches Kissimmee on 23 September 2019.

The old order at Kissimmee. Back in the days of CSX ownership, P42DC #166 arrives at the small station with the southbound Silver Meteor on 19 January 2012. The poor state of the track is evident. This was replaced in 2014, at the same time a new track was added to the right.

A shade under eight years later and the scene has dramatically changed. The track has been doubled, and the new SunRail station, immediately next to the existing Amtrak facility, has opened for business. A northbound service calls at the new platform on 24 September 2019. The crossing just behind the train marks the boundary between new and old.

Ringling Bros. and Barnum & Bailey Circus used rail transport to move themselves and their equipment around the country for virtually their entire existence. The train shown, one of two, is passing northbound through Folkston GA, heading north on 23 January 2012 after spending the winter break in its Florida base.

RBBX 41404, built by Budd in 1955 for the Seaboard Coast Lines, was a sleeper car used for staff accommodation on the 'blue' circus train. Sadly, the circus closed permanently in 2017 after years of falling ticket sales. This car was one of two purchased by the BNSF Railway after closure of the circus.

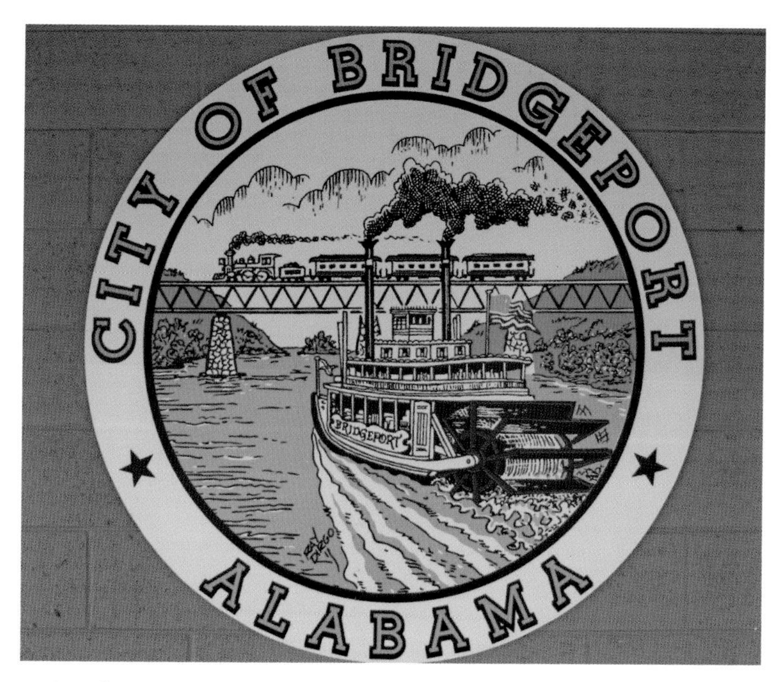

Many US settlements owe at least a part of their history to the railroads. Bridgeport AL is no exception; the railroad crosses the Tennessee River here and has done so since 1854. Whilst the original constructions have been replaced, the original bridge lives on as the centrepiece of the city's crest.

ES40DC #5388 takes a train of auto-racks across the Tennessee at Bridgeport AL on 2 October 2019. The train is on the 1995-built section of the bridge; the old bridge to the right survives as a pedestrian bridge, albeit one that leads to nowhere. The tower peering above the trees is part of the swing section of the bridge which, sadly, is inaccessible for photography.

There are around 212,000 grade crossings in the United States, ranging from farm crossings many miles from the nearest settlements, to multi-lane highways in the metro areas of America's largest cities. This is the southernmost of three crossings in the centre of Folkston GA, with a patiently waiting motorist.

At the other end of town, this driver is rather less patient, zigzagging around the already lowered barriers. On average, there is an accident involving a crossing user and a train every three hours somewhere in the US. In 2016, there were 255 fatalities and 852 serious injuries as a result of crossing misuse.

Just a few moments later and ES40DC #5333 is at the crossing. The US railroad industry has a major safety promotion campaign, Operation Lifesaver, to try to tackle the problem of crossing misuse. This campaign has had some success with casualty figures gradually falling.

Standing over the track of the CSX Montgomery to Mobile main line at Flomaton AL is this 1943-built coaling stage. Constructed by the Louisville and Nashville Railroad, it probably only enjoyed around twelve years or so of active service as most of America's trunk railroads were using diesel traction by the mid-1950s.

Ex-Conrail GP38-2 #2768 brings a local train into the small yard at Flomaton on 7 October 2019. The Class III Alabama Railroad meets CSX tracks here. Now owned by Pioneer Railcorp, the line is currently out of use.

A long northbound manifest train passes under the coaling stage as it snakes through Flomaton on the same day. Note the mid-train DPU (distributed power unit). This unit is provided to assist with steep grades. With less mountainous terrain, the practice is less common in the eastern US than further west.

With the crew about to finish duty, GP38-2 #2768 and train park up in the yard at Flomaton. The locomotive was built in 1977 and entered the Conrail fleet as #8179. The unit passed to CSX in 1999 as part of the division of Conrail between the company and the Norfolk Southern Railroad.

Not far behind the local was this southbound manifest led by ES44AH #923. The Evolution series locomotives are renowned for being strong and reliable and the terrain in the area is relatively flat, but being in solitary control, the locomotive will still have some hard work ahead.

ES44AH #3168 bursts through Flomaton AL earlier the same afternoon. The photograph is taken in the middle of the triangular junction with the tracks to Pensacola FL. The city lies just north of the Florida-Alabama state line.

Waycross GA is a major hub for the CSX system with five lines converging on the city as well as a classification yard and locomotive storage and maintenance facilities. This train, led by rebuilt GP40-3 #6556, is approaching on the former Atlantic Coast Line from the north-east via Jesup. The train is destined for Rice Yard, less than a mile away. 8 October 2019.

Busy triple tracks lead in from the south-east. This is the route from Florida via the Folkston Funnel. This train of auto-racks is signalled to take the route north-west towards Atlanta. Traffic was a little quiet on the evening of 8 October 2019, but it is often possible to see the headlights of the next arrival in the distance.

The crew of ES40DC #5455 have turned off the headlights as they wait beyond a grade crossing for a path across town on 8 October 2019. This route approaches from the north-west via Douglas.

Passing discarded ties from recent track renewal, AC4400CW #61 leads an ES40DC and a train of auto-racks into Waycross from the south-east. These car-carrying wagons were originally built as bi-level cars. More recent versions use lightweight aluminium rather than steel and can be converted to tri-level if required.

A Union Pacific train of oil tanks thunders through the complex junctions at the eastern end of Rice Yard on 8 October 2019, passing a CSX local reversing into the sidings. CSX crew will be operating the train on this section of the long run from Florida to Illinois.

Traffic demands are very seasonal and American Railroads often store locomotives for short periods when demand is lower. Waycross is one of several locations that provide storage facilities. 19730-built GP38-2 #2646 was amongst the storage lines on 27 September 2019.

Two SD40-3 units lead a manifest from the south into Waycross on 8 October 2019. Use of smaller units such as these on this type of duty is still common on the CSX system. Other railroads now generally use high-horsepower units on most long-distance work.

ES44AH #898 and ET44AH #3375 arrive into Waycross on 27 September 2019 with another train of racks from the north. The car visible is a more recent version constructed of aluminium, the orange livery denoting that it is a BNSF-owned car.

Looking like they are ready and waiting for their next duty, these locomotives are actually in store in the yard on 27 September 2019. The SD40-2, #8042, may be a candidate for conversion to SD40-3 specification. The two CW40-8s are more likely to be retired from CSX service.

The track from Jesup crosses the main CSX track through Waycross on a flat crossing as it approaches Rice Yard. GP40-2 #6983 and its Road Slug mate, #2383, back their train over the tracks and into the yard on 27 September 2019. The train had arrived from behind the photographer.

The CSX facility at Waycross occupies a huge swathe of land on the south-west side of town. The track layout has been optimised to take advantage of this and it is possible to route trains from any direction to any other. This five-unit train has arrived from the north-west and is now curving south-west to arrive at Rice Yard.

With the signal in front clearing, the engineer opens up and SD40-3s #s 4010 and 4012 get their train moving on 26 September 2019. On this approach to Waycross, trains sit back from red signals to avoid blocking a grade crossing.

In contrast with the previous few pictures featuring manifest trains, this one has modern, high-horsepower units in charge. ET44AH #3339 and ES44AH #706 round onto the tracks to the south-east on 27 September 2019. After clearing the junctions, the train pushed back on the middle left tracks into Rice Yard.

After and before. The lead locomotive, SD40-3 #4025, is a rebuild of SD40-2 #8184. The second locomotive is an SD40-2, #8368, itself a rebuild from an original SD40 series unit. Many of CSX's SD40 family of units have now completed forty or more years of service and had at least one, if not two, rebuilds.

It is unlikely that these SD70ACs will be quite so lucky as the SD40s. Surplus to requirements after the implementation of Precision Scheduled Railroading, these two units photographed on 27 September 2019 are unlikely to see CSX use again.

Occupying a small corner on the eastern extreme of Rice Yard, Waycross Recycling are a metals company that specialise in the rebuilding of small-yard power. The company premises were seen on 27 September 2019, with five units in various stages of rebuilding.

CSX hosts Amtrak long-distance services on parts of its network. The northbound Silver Star gets underway from Tampa Union station on 1 June 2011. This service will use CSX track for over 80 per cent of its 1,100-mile journey from Miami to New York, swapping to Amtrak-owned infrastructure at Washington DC.

The Amtrak Auto Train, a car- and passenger-carrying service from Lorton VA to Sanford FL, is a notable Amtrak success, but it relies almost entirely on CSX track to make its daily run in each direction. Amtrak GE B32-8WH #515 switches cars at the Sanford terminal in Central Florida. The full train loads to around forty-five passenger cars and auto-racks.

Led by 'bloody nose' liveried P42DC #156, the northbound Silver Meteor service approaches Folkston GA in the hazy gloom of last light on 23 January 2012. The livery is a re-creation of the 1972 Phase 1 colours, applied to celebrate Amtrak's fortieth anniversary in 2011.

After a brief stop, the southbound Silver Meteor leaves its Kissimmee FL call on 24 September 2019. Unusually, the train is led by P42DC #205 and earlier P40DC #816. Now owned by the Florida Department of Transport, the line here was formerly part of the CSX 'A' line.

Seen at Seville FL, the northbound Auto Train of 25 September 2019 is a little over an hour into its sixteen-hour trek north to Lorton VA, a short distance south of Washington DC. A designated small fleet of P40DC units maintain the service, four of which are required each day.

Half an hour further north and locomotives 830 and 832 pass through Pomona Park FL. The forty-four P40DC units entered service with Amtrak in 1993, of these fifteen remain, now running as P42DCs – the other units were retired and sold. Replacement of these locomotives with new Siemens Charger SC-44s is due from 2021.

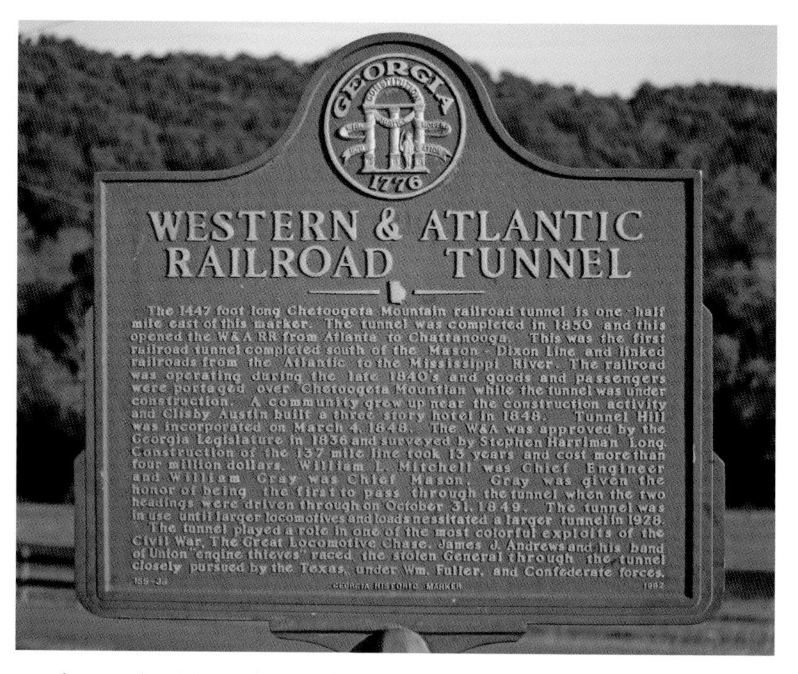

The marker at the CSX rail tunnel at Tunnel Hill GA tells the colourful story of the Western and Atlantic Railroad's 1850 Chetoogeta Mountain Tunnel and its replacement, built in 1928 by the Nashville, Chattanooga and St Louis Railroad. It is possible to walk through the original tunnel at certain times.

Sadly, no train arrived having passed through the tunnel, but the sheer size of the trucks and the locomotives leading them gives an understanding of how tall the US loading gauge is. The original NC&StL tunnel is to the right, obstructed by the trees and signal bridge.

DOTX 219 is a track geometry inspection car belonging to the Federal Railroad Agency. Capable of self-propulsion or being hauled, the car measures every aspect of track geometry and uses high-accuracy GPS equipment to detail any points needing attention. The car is on CSX track at Tunnel Hill GA on 2 October 2019.

A quiet evening in Tunnel Hill GA finds ES44AH #746 leading AC4400CW #211 south towards Dalton on 1 October 2019. Traffic levels on this usually busy stretch were low at the time; this was the only movement through the town in over three hours.

Back on the former CSX 'A' line in Florida and southbound auto-racks arrive at the site of the former Sanford Amtrak station on 31 May 2011. The station closed in August 2005. Behind is the Amtrak Auto Train terminal, and a new SunRail station opened nearby in 2014, providing regular services to Orlando and Poinciana.

Amtrak B32-8WH #508 switches the Sanford Auto Train terminal on 25 September 2019. One of a fleet of twenty units new in 1991, these locomotives saw some years of passenger service with Amtrak before replacement by new Genesis locomotives around the turn of the century. The track behind the unit is that of the CSX Aloma Spur.

Despite the sale of this part of the 'A' line, CSX continues to operate a small yard at Sanford. On 29 May 2011, prior to the sale, GP38-2 #2641 rests in the yard with a single tank car for company. The new Sanford SunRail station now occupies the far southern end of the site.

1998-built AC4400CW #308 in the YN2 'Bright Future' livery passes the yard at Sanford on 12 October 2010. The train is about to pass under State Route 46. This provides access to the new Sanford station from the city and the I-4 Interstate.

A small portion of the southern end of the yard was sacrificed to provide space for the new station, along with parking and a bus terminal. Evidence of the remodelling is still apparent in this view of Sanford Yard taken on 25 September 2019. ES44AH #3035 has just dropped a few hopper cars into the yard.

Moving north-west to Cordele GA and the Sunday morning peace is momentarily disturbed by a three-unit coal train led by ET44AH #3352. The line has several grade crossings as it passes through town, but they are 'no horn' crossings and the familiar four tones are not heard.

On hand at Cordele for local freight workings, the services of GP40-2 #6348 are not needed and the locomotive enjoys the sunset of 28 September 2019. Cordele lies on the tracks of three railroads. Along with CSX, the Norfolk Southern and Genesee and Wyoming-owned Heart of Georgia Railroads pass through.

With a passing track located just to the east, this manifest train travelling in the opposite direction arrived in Cordele soon after the coal train had passed. ES44AH #3068 is in sole charge of the train – the expected mid-train DPU was not present. Pictured on 29 September 2019.

AC4400CW #61 rumbles over the diamond at Cordele on 29 September 2019. This is the intersection of CSX and Norfolk Southern tracks. The track in the foreground provides a link between the two companys' tracks. The condition of the track suggests the link still sees use.

By the next morning, GP40-2 #6348 had moved and been attached to a short consist transferring from the Heart of Georgia Railroad. At sunset, the train had not moved, indicating that it was probably a Monday morning job for the local crew to attend to. 29 September 2019.

A northbound approaches Vienna GA, a few miles north of Cordele, a little later in the day on 29 September 2019. Led by #936, a 2008 ES44AH, the train will parallel US Highway 41 into Vienna before veering north-west and following State Route 90 towards Montezuma and Oglethorpe.

Dominating the skyline of Cordele, the castellated water tower stands adjacent to the CSX Railroad tracks. Built around 1900, the tower has been disused since the 1970s, but is preserved and upkept by the city, who hope to turn the tower into a tourist attraction.

In a haze of brake dust, ES44AH #3218 takes the rear of a train away from the crossings of Cordele. The diamond closest to the train is the tracks of the Norfolk Southern. The second diamond is that of the Heart of Georgia Railroad. Closest to the camera is the curve that links the CSX and NS systems.

North again from Vienna and locomotive #936 roars through Lilly with its northbound consist. The train crosses Highway 90 here, the photographer taking advantage of the lull of traffic on the road to improve the angle of the picture. 29 September 2019.

Looking the other way from the previous picture, the grade crossing and the impressive water tower make the view as ES44AH #740 takes a train of intermodal boxes through Lilly GA on 29 September 2019. A train such as this, with just one locomotive, would be notable elsewhere but seems quite common on the CSX system.

A little further north at Byromville and Highway 90 and the railroad cross once again, this time by means of this rather low-looking bridge. Despite ceasing to exist over a half century ago, the initials of the Atlantic Coast Lines Railroad continue to adorn the bridge. ES44AH #740 crosses on 29 September 2019.

Seen earlier, ES44AH #936 is now just south of Montezuma GA. Here, the train will veer west and cross the tracks of the Norfolk Southern before resuming a northbound course through Oglethorpe towards Manchester GA. Note the flat trucks of military hardware being conveyed on a general manifest service.

A few moments later and #936 and train approaches a crossing with Highway 90 once more, this time in Montezuma. From here, the Norfolk Southern briefly parallels the CSX tracks before the two railroads cross, the CSX line resuming its north-westerly course and the NS continuing south-west.

Another 10 miles north-west and the tracks pass through Ideal. A typical small-town settlement, the city of Ideal once boasted its own railroad station, very much a status symbol back in the late nineteenth century. ES44AH #958 takes a southbound manifest under Highway 90 on 30 September 2019.

Facing the opposite direction and photographed from the bridge in the previous picture, ET44AH #3329 passes the site of the closed station at Ideal GA on 29 September 2019. A passing track lies out of sight around the corner – the train had waited for a southbound service to pass.

Newly re-laid track takes the weight of ES44AH #740 and a relatively short intermodal train as they approach Ideal GA on 29 September 2019. The number boxes in the nose end are more typically placed above the windscreens on this model of the Evolution locomotives.

Further north on the same line, the steep grade into Talbotton GA for southbound trains is evident as ES44AH #816 leads an intermodal towards the passing track located in the town. Note the double-stacked boxes towering over the locomotive. 30 September 2019.

The height of those containers becomes evident as #816 breasts the summit a few moments later. The blue protrusion on the top container is a refrigeration unit. This type of box is used for transportation of chilled or frozen produce. Talbotton GA, 30 September 2019.

A surprise in the same consist was the use of a mid-train helper in the form of ES44AH #3022. In other areas of the US, a loco mid-train on an intermodal service would be an unusual sight. The extra power was needed for the train which passed at little more than walking pace.

The Georgian city of Manchester lies a dozen or so sinuous track miles further north. In common with many other similar locations the city has built an observation deck for railfans to watch the trains roll by. Seen from that deck, AC4400CW #417 waits for a crew to head for Birmingham AL on 30 September 2019.

Tilford Yard in Atlanta GA is the destination of this northbound manifest powering north from Manchester through the town of Gay GA on 30 September 2019. ES44AH #916, one of a batch of 150 Evolutions delivered to CSX in 2008, takes the train slowly over freshly laid track.

Mobile AL is a major traffic centre for both CSX and the Norfolk Southern. Each railroad has a yard, and both access the Gulf Coast Docks. A quiet Sunday afternoon sees ES44AH #786 pass one of the dockyard's multi-storey car parks with a train headed for former Mobile and Montgomery Railroad tracks north.

Deep in the docklands, the minivan has just delivered the crew of this Herzog ballast train for another shift. Train preparation work will soon commence to ensure that ES44AH #709 and the train are fit to travel. Minivans are used extensively to transport crews to and from trains that require relief away from a depot.

A few minutes later and preparation is done. The engineer has fired up the locomotives, handbrakes are released, systems, wheels and pipe connections checked; the train is coupled together and ready to move. The crew will now await instructions from the despatcher via radio before moving to the starting position of the ballast drop.

Two and a half hours later, the train passes its origin point, dropping ballast as it heads west. Herzog trains use a GPS-based system to control ballast drops. As they travel along at low speed a computer opens and closes the chutes to regulate the flow of stone. Pictures from 6 October 2019.

A mid-morning manifest trails into the dockland scenery at Mobile AL on 7 October 2019. A mid-train ES44AC is cut into the formation next to some oil tanks. This practice would at one time have been frowned upon and the locomotive would more likely have been placed between the boxcars.

ES40DC #5412 curves through the heavy industry situated in Mobile Docks on 6 October 2019. The local police department's lock-up is situated just a few yards away. This has resulted in a proliferation of bail bond offices appearing amongst the factories and foundries.

The Herzog ballast train seen earlier was held back to allow this service to pass. Such workings operate at low speed and require careful timing to ensure they do not impede the progress of scheduled traffic. This trio of units, led by ES44AH #798, passed around half an hour in front of the ballast train.

Along with the factories, cranes and bail bond offices, the docklands are littered with grade crossings. Many are literally just dirt tracks, but with trucks frequently crossing, the railroads make protecting their trains a priority. 6 October 2019.

The autumn of 2019 was notably hot and sticky for the southern states with early October temperatures in the high eighties. It was not all sunshine though; the afternoon of 5 October 2019 saw over 2 inches of rainfall in around three hours. The results of a thorough soaking are clear to see as ES44AH #710 draws to a stand close to the yard office at Montgomery AL in fast-fading light.

The next morning, it was hard to tell that the previous afternoon was an almost total washout. Blue skies and warm sun greet ET44AH #3303 and two further units as they as they arrive at Mobile Yard on 6 October 2019. The train drew up to the depot to change crew.

After the crew change, #3303 headed out downtown with its consist. The sloping roof on the right of the picture is the train shed of the former Montgomery Union station. Passenger service to Union ended in 1979 with the discontinuation of the Floridian, the one-time South Wind service from Chicago to Miami.

Before the rainstorm, ES44AH #3057 and AC4400CW #413 passed through Montgomery as light engines, presumably heading for the diesel shed nearby. Behind, the Alabama River snakes past the railroad. The river lets out into the Gulf of Mexico. 5 October 2019.

The 600-foot-long gabled roof of Union station opened in 1898. Built by the Louisville and Nashville, the shed housed six tracks and hosted trains from the Southern Railway as well as the L&N service. The buildings are now commercial office space and the shed now houses rubber-tyred vehicles rather than ones with steel.

Seen the next day in Mobile, ES44AH #709 and AC4400CW #474 set out from Montgomery with the Herzog ballast train during a brief respite from the rain. This was a positioning movement; the train was berthed overnight in Mobile before setting out late afternoon to drop stone. 5 October 2019.

The small diesel shop at Montgomery AL on 5 October 2019. The sidings host a variety of motive power including high-horsepower units. SD40-3 #4010, visible on the right, was seen in Waycross GA nine days earlier, demonstrating the wide operating range the locomotives have.

Before drawing up to the office area to change crew, ES44AH #710 and train were held back by the end of the yard. This would avoid the train blocking a grade crossing for a prolonged period if the relieving crew were not ready to take charge. Puddles fill the former industrial siding space alongside the track.

A final view of Montgomery Union and its fine roof, with the two units lined-up for the Herzog ballast train in picture. The locomotives were in the process of transferring from the diesel shop to the yard containing the ballast hoppers and their loading area.

Showing the current CSX locomotive livery to good effect, ET44AH #3432 is at the rear of a northbound train of hoppers passing through Dalton GA on 1 October 2019. Dalton is another town that provides a viewing area for railfans to watch trains from.

Dalton GA is another city where CSX and the Norfolk Southern directly cross each other's tracks. The diamond directly in front of SD50-3 #8609 provides the crossing point. Besides the preserved passenger coach lies the former station building. Passenger service here ceased nearly fifty years ago.

Situated opposite the Amtrak station, this impressive viewing platform has been constructed by the city of Jesup GA. The city was also involved in the restoration of the 1903-built original Atlantic Coast Lines station after purchase from CSX. Florida-bound freight passes on 27 September 2019.

CW44AH #5104 and AC4400CW #67 both disturb the peace as they approach the city of Rebecca in rural Georgia on 28 September 2019 leading an eastbound manifest train. The speed limit sign is intended for the adjacent Highway 90, not the railroad!

Taken further back along Highway 90, a proliferation of signage is revealed around the grade crossing and intersection with Highway 112. ES44AH #3186 was hard on the heels of the train in the previous shot, approaching Rebecca GA on 28 September 2019.

An out-of-the-way town, the city of Rebecca sounds grand, but the city has a population that has shrunk to fewer than 200 inhabitants. The two greatest constructions in town are the grain silos and the huge signal bridge that controls the westbound exit from the passing track. #3186 passes east.

In typical lush Alabama greenery, the CSX route south through from Decatur to Birmingham is close to Highway 31 for many miles and allows the photographer to picture one train in several locations. Also seen in the first picture, ES44AH #3101 is 20 miles further north at Lacon on 4 October 2019.

Travelling north towards Decatur, the city of Falkville welcomes ET44AH #3304 leading a manifest train on 4 October 2019. Many of the grade crossings on minor roads rise to the tracks. The no trucks rule is applied as there is a risk of a long vehicle grounding as it crosses.

With three star-spangled banners in view, Falkville is a typical Alabamian town, patriotic and well presented. The Louisville and Nashville Railroad opened a station in the town in 1872 and Interstate 65 provides the eastern boundary. On the rear of the same train is ET44AH #3436.

The train made a slow pass of the town. Up ahead the southbound service seen at Lorton with locomotive #3101 in charge was arriving at the other end of the passing track to the left of locomotive #3436. Whilst the grade crossings are activated by the train, the dispatcher controlling the modern signalling could be hundreds of miles away.

Lying just over the state line from the state capital of Florida, Tallahassee, Thomasville GA still supports its own rail yard, situated in the south-west corner of town. With business looking quite healthy, ex-Conrail GP38-2 #2762 switches trucks on 8 October 2019.

Famous to railfans the world over, the Folkston Funnel is the point at which the two CSX routes from the north converge before passing into Florida. The city of Folkston is very railfan friendly and has provided this viewing area, complete with lighting, grills, Wi-Fi and radio tuned to the appropriate railroad channel.

Traffic through the town can vary, both by season and by day; but as an average, thirty freight trains pass daily. There are also six scheduled Amtrak trains per day. Maintenance windows can play havoc with schedules, but experience suggests the busiest time of day is from 2 p.m. to 8 p.m. ES44AH #832 passes on an intermodal turn.

The tracks split the town in two with three grade crossings cutting over the tracks. Martin Street is pictured. The southernmost and quietest of the three, this leads into a residential area. CW44AH #5118 leads a northbound train across on 26 September 2019.

A pair of rather battered-looking C40-8W locomotives with #7686 leading head south through Folkston with a train from Waycross on 23 January 2012. Built in the early 1990s, C40-8W units are now in decline with CSX and the rear unit, #7854, is now owned by General Electric Locomotive Leasing.

An ex-Louisville and Nashville SD40-2 heads an eclectic mix of locomotives north through Folkston, again seen in January 2012. #8069 dates from 1979. Many of these locomotives have now either been uprated to SD40-3s or retired from CSX service.

A rearward view gives a better perspective of the units. Behind SD40-2 #8069 is SD60M #8771. None of this type of locomotive remain with CSX. Borrowed in from the Union Pacific is SD70M #4245, one of over 1,500 such units on the UP roster. Finally, #4654 is a Ferromex ES44AC. Ferrocarril Mexicano is the largest private operator in Mexico.

ES40DC #5377 lifts a relatively short (by US standards) intermodal train over the pronounced hump in the track at Martin Street crossing on 17 January 2012. The train has a few boxes at the front but is otherwise made up of both spine and well cars conveying 'piggyback' road semi-trailers.

Working with #5377 was a former celebrity, C40-8 #7489. Built in 1989, this former Conrail locomotive was one of the last units to carry the blue and white livery of its previous owner and had been repainted only around four months prior to this picture. The locomotive was retired from CSX service in 2016.

As with many American cities, the water tower in Folkston is a local landmark, generally used for self-promotion or perhaps to highlight the local sports team. Folkston's tower is central to the town – the brick building in front is the US Post Office. Dash 9 #9016 passes on 26 September 2019. This is another type of locomotive that is disappearing from the CSX fleet.

Only the front two units of this five-locomotive lash-up are under power; the three smaller locos behind ES40DC #5253 and AC4400CW #162 have been consisted to the train purely for transfer purposes. Heading south through Folkston, the train would be heading for Baldwin Yard near Jacksonville FL, around 30 miles distant.

Two trains meet on the Main Street grade crossing on 17 January 2012. This is the middle of the three crossings and the busiest for road traffic. These two passing at the same time will considerably reduce the waiting time for road users. Pictured on 17 January 2012, the two Dash 8s on the right are now retired.

Under grim skies, two YN2 'Bright Future' liveried units pass with northbound auto-racks on 9 October 2019. As the years pass, more and more YN2-liveried units pass through the paint shop or are retired, making pairings of older-coloured locomotives less and less common.

A welcome sight in 2019 is a pair of SD40-3 units on main-line duty, not something seen anymore in many parts of the country. #s 4023 and 4063 bring a long manifest into Folkston on 9 October 2019. Its likely destination is Waycross, around 25 miles north-east.

Much of the 25 miles to Waycross borders the Okefenokee National Wildlife Reserve, an area of typical south-eastern USA forests and swamps. The tracks are parallel to US Highway 23 but lie largely unseen by road traffic as they are hidden in a long, tree-lined grove. #5238, a 2005 ES40DC, leads a manifest train on 27 September 2019.

Back in downtown Folkston, another now retired C40-8W unit, #7310, brings another load of hoppers in from the Waycross sub on 17 January 2012. This was one of a batch of sixty locomotives delivered to Conrail, all of which passed to CSX in the Conrail split. None survive in CSX service in 2020.

Looking very much as it did when delivered twenty-three years previously, AC4400CW #117 drifts through Folkston on 26 September 2019. Time may not be on the side of the locomotive. Higher-horsepower units such as these tend to average a service life of around twenty to twenty-five years with the Class I railroads.

The orange and white containers of two of the largest shipping companies in the US, JB Hunt and Schneider National, are briefly broken by mid-train DPU ET44AH #3312, passing over the Main Street crossing on 26 September 2019. The equipment of both companies can be seen in virtually every corner of the US.

On the same remarkably busy afternoon, ES44AH #881 and ES40DC #5492 cross Main Street heading south on what is nominally the northbound track. Multiple-track routes controlled by the latest signalling equipment are generally bi-directionally signalled. This is of great assistance to operations in times of disruption or maintenance.

Connecting with CSX at Bridgeport AL, the Sequatchie Valley Railroad runs over the state line to Jasper TN, some 12 miles distant. The line continued further north to Dunlap TN in the Louisville and Nashville Railroad era. This was cut back to the present terminus in the 1990s. EMD SW1500 #Y1205 and GP40-2 #3002 rest at Bridgeport on 2 October 2019.

Conrad Yelvington Distributors Inc. use this GP30M at their rock facility located alongside the site of the former Amtrak station at Sanford FL. CYXX 2105 started life with the Baltimore and Ohio Railroad in 1962 as a GP30, and passed to present ownership via the Chessie System, CSX and the Alabama and Gulf Coast Railroad.

The 350-mile Florida East Coast Railway makes a connection with the CSX system on the north shore of the St John's River at Jacksonville FL. Designated as a Class II Regional Railroad, the company operates Bowden Yard, a couple of miles south of downtown. With the city in the distance, the yard is doing good business on 24 January 2012.

Seen in the previous picture, this FEC train is heading south away from Jacksonville on the same day. EMD SD70M-2 #106 leads #140, an identical unit owned by Citirail Leasing, and GP40-2 #431, new to the Florida East Coast in 1984. FEC rails end in Miami Port but at one time stretched across The Keys to Key West.

BNSF trains bring coal from the Wyoming coalfields into the deep south, crewed and operated by CSX personnel whilst on CSX rails. BNSF SD70ACe #8537 leads a loaded train across the Tennessee River at Decatur AL on 3 October 2019.

This Union Pacific oil train at Waycross GA is worked by a similar method, with CSX crew in the cab. Note the barrier wagons between locomotives and tanks, a formation not used by CSX. AC4400CW #6712 gets underway after a signal stop on 8 October 2019.

Norfolk Southern ET44AC #3627 brings BNSF coal over the Tennessee River at Bridgeport AL on 2 October 2019. The line is CSX owned, but the Norfolk Southern have trackage rights from Chattanooga TN to Stevenson AL from where they continue south-west to Decatur AL whilst CSX veers north for Nashville TN.

Far from home, two Canadian National units drop railcars off at a facility in Auburndale FL on 24 September 2019. The effects of 2019's hot summer continuing long into the autumn are apparent – by this time of year rainfall would normally be increasing and temperatures starting to fall.

The two Canadian National units reform their train out on the running line before heading towards Lakeland and Tampa. The Class Is frequently lend each other traction, but the lead locomotive, SD70M-2 #8894, is an unusual choice as CSX do not own or operate any of the type.

The Norfolk Southern and CSX railroads meet in many places and trackage agreements exist between the two. A visit from the Federal Railroad Agency's track recording cars will almost certainly mean one company will end up on the other's track. Norfolk Southern SD70ACe #1096 runs on CSX rails at Tunnel Hill GA.

The Florida Central Railroad operates a 70-mile system in Lake and Orange Counties north-east of Orlando, and exchanges with CSX at Taft Yard, south of Orlando Amtrak. A 1959 vintage GP9 originally owned by the Norfolk Western is fuelled at the railroad's Plymouth maintenance facility on 26 January 2012.

CSX units can be seen far from their normal territory on occasion. These two units are being led by BNSF ES44C4 #6657 on Union Pacific tracks at Caliente CA on 11 February 2015. It is likely that the train originated at a military facility directly served by CSX and the locomotives will work the train to destination.

Another locomotive type destined to end CSX service soon is the GE C40-9W. Also known as Dash 9's, these locomotives date from the early 1990s and are one of the forerunners of the successful Evolution series locomotives. #9021 still carries its original YN2 colours at Dawson NE on 7 October 2015.

Seen with Union Pacific SD70ACe #8695 and patched former Southern Pacific AC44CW #6400, #9021 is on secondment to the Union Pacific at Dawson NE. Whilst the old CSX livery remains a common sight, the Southern Pacific black and orange is now becoming a rarity as older units are repainted or, in some cases, retired.

The BNSF yards at Clovis lie alongside the busy Southern Transcon. This long cross-country route receives traffic of all types from all corners of the country, and as a result foreign motive power will often end up far from its home system. Two CSX units are seen enjoying the New Mexico climate on 28 October 2017.

Seen to the left in the previous picture, the BNSF-NS-CSX lash-up has now drawn forward with a fresh crew in charge and will shortly return to its westbound course across the New Mexico desert. The foreign units will now almost certainly end up in California, around 2,500 miles from home.

Another of the few surviving 'patch' former Southern Pacific AC44CWs, #6379, accompanies CSX ES44AH #3166 at Daggett CA on 11 February 2019. This train will have originated in the US Marine Corps base at Yermo, a couple of miles to the north. The train is awaiting a path onto the Southern Transcon towards Barstow.

A line closure at Las Vegas NV caused diversion of Union Pacific trains along the Southern Transcon on 30 January 2017. Seen in the Mojave Desert at Cadiz CA, both UP and CSX locomotives are not often seen at this location. CSX #4780, an EMD SD70MAC, is the middle unit of the three.

This train of BNSF auto-racks, passing Monolith CA on 30 March 2014, is utilising a borrowed CSX ES44DC, #5501. The racks will ultimately go to the San Francisco Bay area to collect imported cars and trucks. The locomotives may also go through if they are not swapped at Bakersfield.

In this final view of CSX in foreign fields, a trio of EMD power is made up by Union Pacific SD70M #5028, CSX SD70MAC #4790 and UP SD70ACe #8685. The maintenance of way train passes Ilmon CA on 11 February 2015. High-horsepower EMD units have lost favour with CSX in recent years; many of the SD70MACs are no longer in service.

Nightfall at Waycross GA on 8 October 2019. ET44AH #3420 drifts through town at last light. The floodlights at Rice Yard and the end of another shift are just in front.